Kitty Capers

15 Quilt Projects with Purrsonality

CAROL ARMSTRONG

C&T PUBLISHING

Text and Watercolor Illustrations
©2006 Carol Armstrong
Artwork ©2006 C&T Publishing, Inc.

Publisher: Amy Marson
Editorial Director: Gailen Runge
Acquisitions Editor: Jan Grigsby
Editor: Liz Aneloski
Technical Editor: Teresa Stroin
Copyeditor/Proofreader: Wordfirm Inc.
Cover Designer: Kristy Zacharias
Production Artist: Kirstie L. Pettersen
Illustrator: Kirstie L. Pettersen
Production Assistant: Kiera Lofgreen
Photography: Luke Mulks and Diane Pedersen,
    unless otherwise noted
Published by C&T Publishing, Inc., P.O. Box
1456, Lafayette, CA 94549

Library of Congress Cataloging-in-Publication Data
Armstrong, Carol,
Kitty capers : 15 quilt projects with purrsonality / Carol
Armstrong.
   p. cm.
ISBN 1-57120-319-2
1. Appliqué--Patterns. 2. Quilting. 3. Cats in art. I. Title.
TT779.A7587 2006
746.46'041--dc22
2005013131

Printed in China
10 9 8 7 6 5 4 3 2 1

CONTENTS

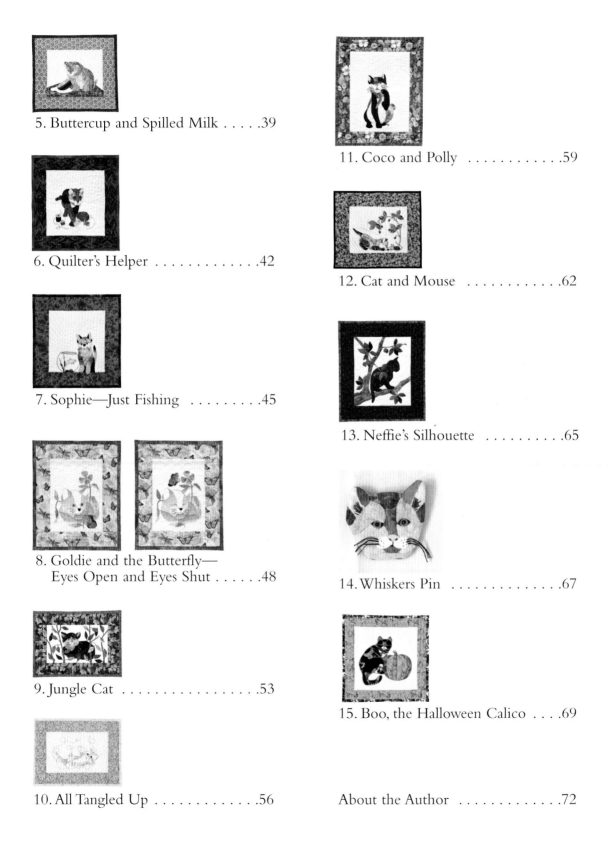

Introduction

Playful and endearing, mischievous and shy, cats and kittens offer endless opportunities for appliqué designs. And what could be more fun? Using my no-fuss lightbox technique for hand appliqué, you too can create vignettes featuring your favorite cat's antics. No need for templates or freezer-paper patterns. Pick a pattern and some fabrics and start sewing! You're sure to find some new accents for your appliqué: eyes made from faux suede, some easy dimensional whiskers, or a little embellishment here and there.

And, of course, there is plenty of space for oodles of background quilting around these simple motifs. A sea of hearts surrounding those sweet newborns, a tangle of curving lines wrapping around a playful knittin' kitten, or a large quilted feather behind a parrot and friend can strengthen a quilt's theme. Simple echo quilting or a random mix of designs can also enrich the texture and please the eye.

So try your hand at some appliqué and quilting. These cat quilts are irresistible and full of smiles!

Supplies

CHAPTER
1

TOOLS

Lightbox: A lightbox allows you to be free of templates. It makes tracing patterns, appliqué pieces, and quilting designs simple. Lightboxes are available in many sizes at craft and art stores. In a pinch, a window on a sunny day will suffice. A low-wattage light under a glass table is also quite functional.

TIP   If you cannot see the black pattern lines through a darker fabric even with a good lightbox, trace over the black lines with a red marker for better visibility.

Cutting Tools: Good sharp scissors, both large and small, are important for efficient cutting of fabric and snipping of threads. For cutting borders, bindings, and backgrounds consider a rotary cutter, mat, and quilter's ruler.

Needles and Pins: Sharp, straight, burr-free pins are needed. Short, ¾″-long glass-head pins are excellent for appliqué. Standard silk pins will serve well for holding borders, bindings, and other basic pieces for stitching.

A long sewing needle speeds up the process of basting quilt layers together.

I use a number 10 milliner's needle for appliqué. The extra length aids in needle-turning the pieces.

Large-eye embroidery needles are easy to thread with floss for adding stitched details. I use sizes 8 to 10.

A number 9 or 10 sharps needle works for my quilting style—no frame or hoop. You may find that a quilting between needle works best for frame quilting.

TIP   When it comes to needle sizes, the larger the number the smaller the needle. For example, a number 10 is smaller than an 8.

Thimble: I use a thimble on the pushing finger when I quilt. A soft, small leather thimble is quite comfortable. Try various styles of thimbles until you find one that works best for your style. They all seem a little awkward in the beginning.

🐾 **Iron:** I like to use some steam when pressing. Use a padded surface for pressing appliqué.

TIP   Press appliquéd pieces from the back.

🐾 **Markers:** My appliqué techniques require removable fabric markers. Water-removable blue markers work very well. There are also white and silver pencils. Investigate the possibilities at your local quilt shop. Always test any marker's removability and follow the package directions. Mark lightly for easier removal.

TIP   A cotton swab dipped in water makes a great "eraser" for water-removable markers.

MATERIALS

🐾 **Thread:** For appliqué, I use a cotton or cotton-wrapped polyester thread in a color to match the appliquéd fabric as closely as possible.

For quilting, I use any of the hand quilting threads available. Natural color to match my unbleached backgrounds is my predominant choice.

For basting, a plain white cotton thread works best.

Embroidery floss of good quality is used for those little details that add so much to your appliquéd designs.

Waxed linen thread makes wonderful dimensional whiskers. Look for this in craft departments. I usually split this thread for thinner whiskers. A carpet thread can also be used, but it is less stiff, so a bit of beeswax is helpful.

🐾 **Batting:** A needle-punched polyester is my favorite. The blanket-like density holds its shape even when closely quilted. Lightweight cotton battings also work well but give a somewhat flatter result.

TIP   Quilt a few little "quiltlets" using various battings for a reference library.

🐾 **Fabric:** My backgrounds are usually unbleached muslin. I use one that is preshrunk and permanent press. I think of the background as my sheet of paper ready for the paint. And my paints are picked from a palette of various print, tone-on-tone, batik, and solid 100% cotton fabrics.

I choose lightweight fabrics that will respond well to being turned under by needle or hand, although if the color is just perfect, I might choose a slightly heavier fabric that can be convinced to cooperate. The more you practice appliqué the easier you will recognize a fabric's character and willingness to be appliquéd, and the better your convincing will be.

To wash? I do not wash my fabrics for wall quilts. If you suspect that a color might bleed, test rinse a small swatch to see if there is any overdye. As quilters, we each have our own preferences. If the finished project will be headed for a bath, you may choose to prewash your fabrics.

Faux suede is the fabric I have used for all the cat eyes, although you can embroider the eyes if you like. This material is nonwoven and accepts pen and paint. Eyes can be colored, cut out, and glued in the eye sockets (pages 16–17). Because I usually color the suede completely with pens, the shade of suede does not matter. A neutral tone is good to use, and a light to medium weight makes for easy handling.

Fabric Color and Print: Well, we need them all, don't we? For cats, put together several shades of a color with some contrast. Try to avoid putting busy prints side by side. One of the design elements of appliqué is the line formed where fabrics meet. Two very busy prints may obscure this line. Audition colors and designs as you cut out your cats. If a cut piece simply doesn't work, it can always be saved for cutting something smaller on another quilt. Look at the printed details in fabric. You may find that a large leaf may be cat fur, indeed! The center of a flower may be a foot pad—aha! Or a soft fern print may really be a soft kitten's coat! Enjoy the exploration.

TIP   Can't find that shade to match another? Do not overlook the reverse side of many fabrics as an option.

Extras: For coloring eyes, I use permanent art pens such as Pigma brand, especially for black. For colors, I like the new gel pens. A touch of white acrylic paint works well for the glint in each eye. Any fabric glue will adhere the eyes in place. (I use Aleene's Tacky Glue.) The scrapbooking section of your craft shop will provide many options for pens, paints, and glues. It is fun trying new products.

Lightbox Appliqué: The Method

I like to keep things simple, and lightbox appliqué does just that. With no templates to prepare or freezer paper to remove, this relaxed method of appliqué lets you get right to the creating. What could be more "purrfect" for these wonderful cats?

PREPARE THE APPLIQUÉ PIECES

Trace your appliqué design on lightweight white paper with a black marker. Secure the drawing on the lightbox with a few pieces of masking tape. If your drawing is larger than your lightbox, tape the pattern to the reverse side of the background fabric instead.

Cut your background fabric at least one inch larger all around than the final size needed. This allows for any drawing up in the fabric. The background will be trimmed to size after the appliqué and embroidery have been completed and the piece is pressed. Lay the background fabric right side up over the drawing on the lightbox. Refer to the project photo to position the appliqué pattern correctly under the fabric. Be sure there is at least 1″ between the pattern and any edge of the background fabric. Secure the fabric to the drawing with a few pins, if you like. Or, if your pattern is taped to the reverse side of your background fabric, move the pattern and background as one to the lightbox. Using a water-removable marker, trace the entire design onto the background. Remove the background from the lightbox but not the pattern. If the pattern is larger than the lightbox, remove the pattern from the back of the background fabric and place the pattern on the lightbox.

Using the pattern on the lightbox, trace each individual appliqué shape, in the exact finished size, onto the right side of each chosen appliqué fabric. This includes those lines that meet other pieces. Use a removable marker in a color that is clearly visible on the fabric. This line will be your guide for turning under the seam allowance. If one piece will overlap another piece, such as a leaf or a stem across a cat leg, mark these areas with a dotted line to aid in the placement of the overlapping pieces.

Cut out the marked pieces ³⁄₁₆˝ to ¼˝ outside the marked line. The allowance can be cut even larger and trimmed as you appliqué if it is in the way. This excess is helpful when there are many overlapping pieces, as with a cat. If a piece shifts a little, the extra fabric is there if needed, or may be trimmed if not.

TIP   If you are appliquéing a light-color piece, you can add a lining to keep the turn-under allowance from showing through. Cut a lining piece the exact finished size of the appliqué (without the turn-under allowance) from a solid color that matches the appliqué fabric. Place the patch behind the appliqué piece and stitch as usual, turning the allowance under between the lining and the background. For a slightly dimensional look you could cut the lining from some thin batting.

APPLIQUÉ ORDER AND STITCHING

Each shape in the patterns is numbered by order of appliqué. The appliqué pieces in the background of a design, those pieces that are covered by another piece, are sewn down first. With some experience, you will easily note the order yourself. Unnumbered pieces or those without overlapping pieces can be sewn at any time.

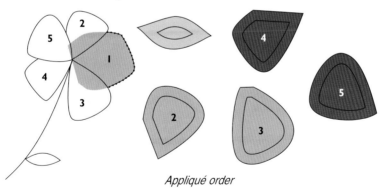

Appliqué order

Begin stitching, using the numbers on the pattern for the order to appliqué. The lines you marked on the background fabric will be your guides. Pre-appliqué where appropriate. Detailed instructions for pre-appliqué begin on page 11. Turn under the allowance with the needle or your finger, matching the line on the appliqué piece with the line on the background, and stitch using the appliqué stitch. Detailed instructions for this stitch begin on page 11. Check often to see that the piece is lined up correctly. For a large appliqué piece, pin the entire piece in place, turning under the allowance here and there to help line it up and to prevent the piece from stretching as you sew. Turn under and sew only those edges that will be exposed, not those that will be covered by another piece. Exception: If you are appliquéing a piece that will be overlapped by a leaf, tail, or any other small piece and the distance is short, turn under the allowance and keep stitching the entire piece, keeping the lines smooth. For example, the pot is completely appliquéd behind the strawberry leaves (page 37) and the cat is completely appliquéd down behind the butterfly (top of page 49).

The markings you have made are removable, so do not worry about the little variations that occur. Those marks will disappear with water after the work is done. Being off a bit on overlapping pieces is fine, as long as all the raw edges are turned or covered by another piece. Remember that the cat may have moved, a bug may have tasted a leaf, or a gentle breeze passing by may have ruffled some fur. Look at your picture as a whole and not at each individual piece. Relax. Close is good. Enjoy the process as much as the finished piece.

When the appliqué is finished, add the eyes and embroider the details, such as whiskers, stems, or butterfly bodies. Detailed instructions begin on page 16 for the eyes and page 19 for the embroidery.

TIP Consider embroidery as separate from appliquéd pieces. When an appliquéd piece abuts to embroidery, such as a butterfly's body, complete the turn-under edge that will meet the embroidery. This will keep any raw edges or threads from coming up through the embroidery stitches.

Remove any visible marks and allow the piece to dry completely. Press the appliqué from the back on a padded surface, using an iron with a bit of steam, set on a cotton setting. Trim the background to the required size.

PRE-APPLIQUÉ

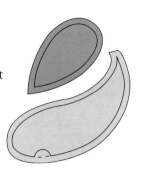

This method of appliqué should be added to everyone's techniques, since it improves the look of many designs and makes turning under the meeting edges smoother and easier. With pre-appliqué, two or more pieces of a motif are sewn to each other before they are applied to the background. I used this technique for most of the cat ears, the two-tone leaves, and the feather; see pages 37 and 61 for some examples. The times to use this method will become easy to spot as you gain appliqué experience.

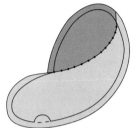

For pre-appliqué; marking, cutting out, and the appliqué stitch are the same as for appliqué, and generally the order of appliqué is the same. Do not stitch into the perimeter turn-under allowance, so it will turn under easily when you appliqué the motif to the background.

Pre-appliqué

Clip curves and trim excess fabric as needed. Remember to match the thread color to the appliqué fabric as you sew. Keep needles threaded and at the ready.

When your pieces are complete, stitch them to the background as one piece.

THE APPLIQUÉ STITCH

Thread a needle with a 12″ to 18″ length of thread in a color to match the appliqué fabric. A longer thread will wear out before you use its entire length. Use only a single strand of thread for appliqué. Knot the end of the thread.

Whenever possible, begin your appliqué at one end of the shape in order to create a continuous line of stitching.

Keep the background fabric somewhat taut as you appliqué to avoid pushing the background fabric as you needle-turn the appliquéd piece. I appliqué on my lap; for most projects the friction of the fabric on my jeans is enough to provide a smooth working background. If the background is small or I am working near an edge, I may pin the background to my jeans or a small lap pillow. Re-pin the background as you sew and need to turn the piece. Pins always provide that extra hand.

Appliqué stitch

Using the shaft of the needle, turn under the edge of the piece at the marked line. Slip the knot into the fold of the turn-under by running the needle through the fold from the back of the appliqué piece and out onto the edge to be stitched down. The knot will be hidden in the fold.

Hold the appliqué in the marked place on the background. Insert the needle into the background at a point even with the thread's exit from the appliqué piece.

With the needle still under the background, move the needle tip forward. Come up through the background and through a few threads on the folded edge of the appliqué piece. Pull the thread snug without drawing up the fabric.

Again, insert the needle into the background even with the thread's last exit point from the turned edge. Travel a bit under the background and come back up through the background, again catching a few threads on the folded edge. Keep folding the turn-under allowance with the shaft of the needle as you go, trimming or clipping as necessary.

To keep your stitching consistent and comfortable, turn your work as you sew. Do not work too far ahead of yourself. Now and then, check that the whole piece will line up with the lines marked on the background. Relax as you stitch. Let the little variations happen and you will create a wonderful appliqué design.

To end, secure the thread by taking three stitches in the same place in the background behind the appliqué, or in an adjacent area of background that will be covered by another appliqué. On your last piece in a motif or a single leaf you will have to go to the back of the work to end the thread with three stitches over each other.

As you sew more and more, your stitches will become small, even, and automatic. Learning what fabric will do when asked takes some practice.

INSIDE POINTS

Using small scissors, clip to the inside point, just shy of the marked turn-under line. Avoid starting at the inside point. Start stitching the piece at a comfortable place that will give you a continuous line of stitching. Stitch almost to the inside point. Using the needle, turn under part of the allowance on the opposite side, down to the clip. Hold in place.

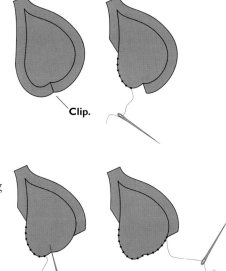

Put the needle under the appliqué and pivot the piece, rolling the allowance under and around the point. Hold the piece in place and stitch to the inside point. Take one or more tiny stitches at the inside point, then adjust the turn-under on the way out of the inside point, smoothing as you sew. Continue stitching around the piece.

Inside points

INSIDE CURVE

Clip the turn-under allowance as many times as needed for a smooth turn-under. Clip to within 1–2 threads before you reach the seamline. When the curves are tight, use the same pivoting needle technique you used for inside points.

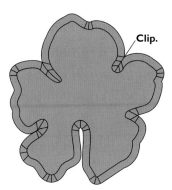

Try to avoid creating tight curves or inside points whenever possible. I recommended a bit of practice on some scrap fabric.

Inside curves

POINTS

Once you have sewn a few points, you will find that they are not as difficult as you thought. The sharper the point, the slower you should sew, carefully easing under the seam allowance. Give a few a try with scrap fabrics.

Square off the end of the point, leaving a ¾6˝ turn-under allowance. If there is too much fabric to turn under, simply trim it. Fold under the allowance straight across the point. Bring your thread up through the exact point, hiding the knot in the fold. Take one stitch into the background.

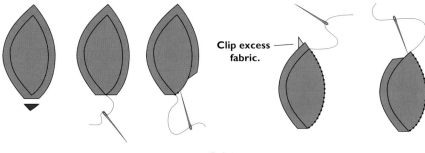

Points

Hold down the end of the appliqué. Using the shaft of the needle, turn under a portion of the allowance beyond the point, then stitch. Continue stitching to the next point. Make a stitch at the exact point on your appliqué shape. Take another tiny stitch to secure the piece if you like. Clip any excess fabric at the point. Push the fabric down to square off the point and, while you are still holding the end down, turn the allowance under on the other side of the point with the shaft of the needle. Continue stitching.

You have now finished a point at the beginning and a point within a line of stitching. All points do not come out perfect. Allow these variations to be part of the whole.

BIAS STRIPS

Use fabric cut on the bias when stitching blades of grass or thin stems or branches. Bias is cut at a 45° angle to the straight grain. It does not fray easily and is flexible enough to go around curves. For a tight curve I stay on the true bias, but for a simple sweeping curve just off-grain is sufficient.

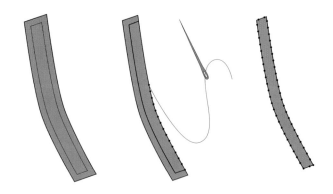

Bias strips

For stitching larger widths of bias, simply cut your bias strip the width of the finished appliqué plus the turn-under allowance on both sides. For example, cut a bias strip 1¼″ wide for a ¾″ finished stem. Turn under the allowance as you sew down one side, stitching the stem in place following the marked lines on the background. Use your needle to turn under the allowance along the other side as you stitch. When it is convenient I stitch the inside edge of a curve first.

TINY BIAS TECHNIQUE

For narrow bias strips, especially for flower and leaf stems, I cut the strip about ½″ wide so it will be easy to work with. As with wider strips, turn under the allowance as you sew down one side. Do not worry too much about the size of the allowance. With one side stitched down, flip the piece open to expose the sewn turn-under allowance and carefully trim the allowance of any extra, but not so close as to weaken the fabric. Flip the piece back and trim it to double the width of the desired stem. Needle-turn the allowance as you stitch down the other side. Some fabrics are more cooperative than others; if one fabric gives you trouble, try another one. You will be surprised how narrow a line you can create with just a little practice.

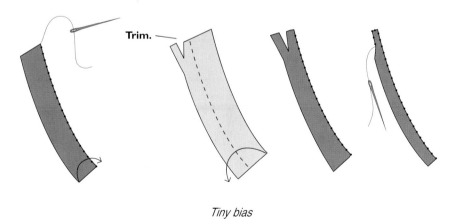

Tiny bias

CAT EYES

Your cat will spring to life when you add the eyes. What fun when your appliquéd pet looks back at you! The eyes can be embroidered, but my choice is to use faux suede.

Embroidered Eyes

As you appliqué, all the edges of the pieces that meet the eye area need to be turned under and stitched down. This creates a socket. Using three strands of floss, satin stitch the eye parts, filling in the space completely. Be sure to add a stitch of white to the pupils to add a spark of life.

Faux Suede Eyes

As you appliqué, all the edges of the pieces that meet the eye area need to be turned under and stitched down. The suede eyes will be added after the quilting is finished. As part of the quilting, quilt around the inside of the eye sockets. Then, using fabric glue, adhere the finished eyes in place. Allow the glue to dry.

To make the eyes, trace the pattern outline onto a piece of paper or card stock.

Cut out the eyes to make a stencil. Using this stencil and a fine-line permanent marker, draw the eye shapes onto the suede by tracing around the inside of the openings.

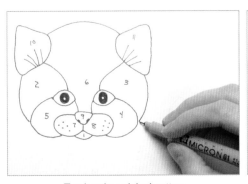
Tracing the original pattern

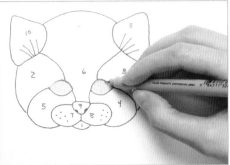
Draw the eye shapes using the stencil.

Remove the stencil.

Referring to the pattern, mark and color the pupil areas in black. Allow this to dry.

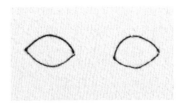
Drawn eye shapes

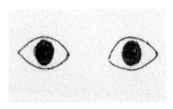
Color the pupil black.

Note that inks are slower to dry on faux suede than on paper. After the black is dry, fill in the rest with a gel pen in the color of your choice. Use more than one shade if you like, for more depth of the eye, or mix colors, such as green and metallic gold. Allow the gel to dry and then add a dot of white acrylic paint, using a toothpick, to give the eyes sparkle and life. Again, allow everything to dry thoroughly.

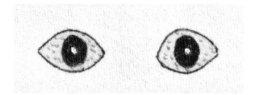

Color the eye and place a dot of white in the center.

Cut out the eyes, trimming them to fit inside the openings formed by the appliqué.

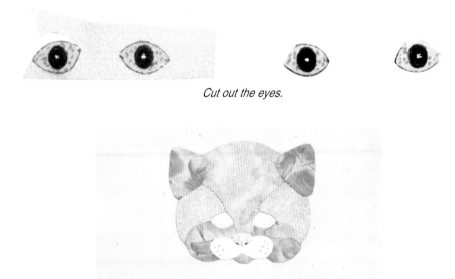

Cut out the eyes.

Appliqué ready for eyes to be glued

After the quilting and binding are finished, glue the eyes in place and allow them to dry. If you trim the eyes a bit shy, color the muslin with a black marker in the eye socket to prevent any white from showing. A Pigma pen is good for this.

Finished face

WHISKERS

Whiskers look great embroidered using the stem stitch and a single strand of embroidery floss. Various colors, from black and brown to white, are suitable for most kitties.

For a dimensional look, waxed linen or carpet thread with a bit of beeswax make adorable whiskers. I split the waxed linen once or twice for thin whiskers.

First, finish all the appliqué and other embroidery and press. Knot a piece of split waxed linen and sew into the back of the fabric behind the cheek; take a backstitch in the background fabric to secure the thread.

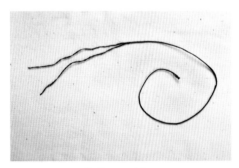

Split waxed linen

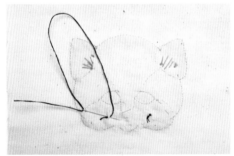

Knot, secure the knot, and backstitch.

TIP Do not iron waxed linen. The heat may cause some of the color to transfer to your fabric.

Then bring the needle through the piece to the front of the cheek where you want the whisker to originate, pulling the full length of the linen through.

Cut off the linen at the length of whisker you choose.

Bring needle to front and pull thread taut.   *Trim thread to whisker length.*

Continue adding these threads one at a time until you like the look—three to five whiskers per cheek. The stiffness of the waxed linen allows you to position the whiskers as you like. What fun to give your cat such personality!

EMBROIDERY

To add those little details that perk up any appliqué, a little simple embroidery is needed. For most details I use two strands, for whiskers I use one, and for large areas to be filled with satin stitch three strands can be used.

French Knot

The French knot is a great flower center and handy whenever you need a dot of color. You can increase the size of the knot by using more strands of floss.

Bring the needle up from the wrong side of the fabric. Wrap the floss around the needle twice and insert the needle back into the fabric close to the thread's exit. Pull the needle through the fabric, holding the knot until all the floss is pulled through. Pull the knot, but not too tightly.

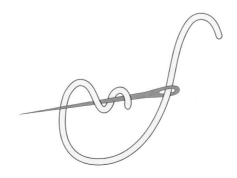

Stem Stitch

This simple stitch outlines and makes delicate whiskers with only one strand of floss. Also, use it for small stems as an alternative to tiny bias. Embroider several parallel lines to make a stem thicker. This stitch is worked left to right.

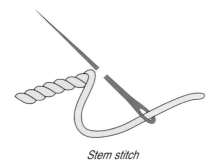

Stem stitch

Satin Stitch

Use this stitch for coloring areas of eyes, for nostrils on little pink noses, or for those cute mouths. It is also good for butterfly bodies and any area you need to fill with color.

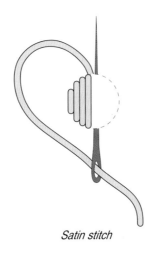

Satin stitch

Borders, Quilting, and Finishing

CHAPTER 3

BORDERS

Borders show off your appliquéd picture just as a frame shows off a painting. Add one or more borders in various widths.

Trim your finished appliquéd piece to the desired size before adding borders. Measure the height of the finished appliquéd piece and trim the side border strips to that size. Be sure the borders opposite each other are the same length. Make sure that any unfinished edges of appliqué on the perimeter of the background will be caught in the stitching when you add the borders. Use a ¼″ seam allowance and stitch the side borders onto the appliquéd piece. Press. Measure and trim the top and bottom border strips. Stitch them to the piece and press. If you add a second border, simply repeat the sequence.

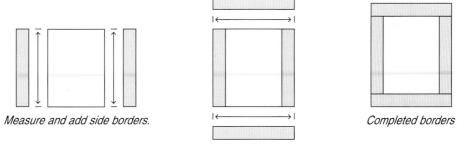

Measure and add side borders.

Measure and add top and bottom borders.

Completed borders

TIP   Use a ¼″ seam allowance for all piecing and borders. Use ½″ when applying binding.

QUILTING

Quilting is like adding a second design to the appliquéd one. The shadows and highlights created by the quilting lines make the background rich and alive. I rarely quilt in the appliqué itself except around some of the larger pieces in the cats to give the cats dimension and to keep the quilt flat. The more random the quilting design, the more fun it can be. Wonderful surprises happen when you combine various shapes and lines of quilting patterns.

Marking

When quilting, I mark as little as possible. The less marking I do, the less I have to remove. The amount of marking you'll need depends on the type of design and your level of experience. For consistency, designs that repeat should be premarked. Do this before you layer your piece with batting and backing. A random or free design can be "eyeballed," just doodling lines with your stitching. Drag the needle across the fabric to create a line that will stay just long enough to quilt. In other words, mark as you go.

Use a water-removable marker and a lightbox to trace the type of quilting designs that need to be premarked. Masking tape comes in many widths and makes a great tool for marking any straight lines. However, do not leave tape on your fabric for an extended period of time. You can also cut templates in any shape from a nonwoven fabric or paper, pin them to the quilt, and stitch around them. The more you quilt, the less you need to mark.

Quilting Designs

The most often asked question is, where do I start my design? Some element or shape in the appliqué may inspire you, such as a leaf or flower. You may wish to highlight the main subject, such as the cat. In that case, begin by quilting a design that surrounds or emanates from the cat. Give the piece a mood with radiating lines of sun or soft loops of clouds. Echo anything or add feathers in the background. The ideas are endless, as are the combinations of those ideas. To get you started, each project in this book has suggestions and ideas. Jot down ideas as you get them, to have on hand next time you are scratching your head and looking for something new.

BASTING THE LAYERS

This important step helps keep your quilt smooth and flat during and after quilting. Cut the batting and backing 1″ or more larger than the top on all sides. Lay out the backing right side down on a smooth, hard surface that will not be harmed by a needle. A cutting mat is great for this purpose.

Add the batting and then the quilt top, with the right side up. Keep the layers smooth and flat. Using white thread and a large needle, baste a grid of horizontal and vertical lines about 4″ apart using 1″-long stitches. The basted grid keeps everything in place as you quilt.

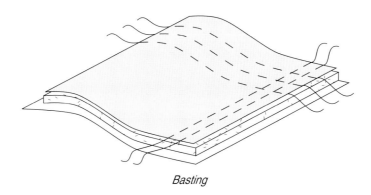

Basting

GETTING STARTED WITH QUILTING

I quilt in my lap without a frame. I find this method works best for me. I use a simple running stitch for quilting and take several stitches on the needle each time.

To begin, knot a 12″ to 18″ length of quilting thread. Too long a piece will wear out before you use it all. Pull the knot through the top when using muslin, pull the knot through the back on colored fabrics to prevent threads from coming loose. Come up to the top of the quilt. Trust the basting and do not push or pull the layers as you quilt. Allow the quilt to relax as you sew. Be sure to catch all three layers in the stitches.

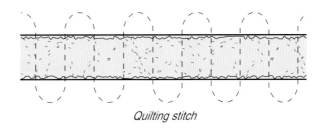

Quilting stitch

I tend to rock the fabric more than the needle, holding the needle against my middle finger with a thimble and feeding the fabric onto the needle.

To end a thread, knot the thread close to the quilt top and pull it into the batting. Let the needle travel between the layers an inch or so, then come up with the needle and snip the thread. The tail left in the batting helps secure the thread. As in the beginning, do this on the back if you end a thread in colored fabric.

BINDING

Binding is the finishing touch for your quilt. I use a straight single-fold crossgrain binding. To make this binding, cut 2″- to 2¼″-wide binding strips from selvage to selvage, using a rotary cutter, ruler, and mat. Measure and trim the binding strips using the same method as for borders (page 21). They are sewn onto the quilt in the same order as the borders: first the sides, then the top and bottom. Stitch the binding to the quilt using a ½″ seam allowance. This results in a ½″-wide finished bound edge.

After the quilt is quilted and before binding it, trim the backing and batting flush with the border's edge, making sure the piece is square.

Following the illustration, turn the binding to the back and fold under the raw edge twice to create a ½″ binding on the front. Miter the corners. Pin the entire binding in place before stitching it down on the back. Blind stitch it down, being careful not to let any of your stitches go through to the front. I prefer to sew my binding on completely by hand for a consistent look with all the other hand sewing. Always sign and date your quilt.

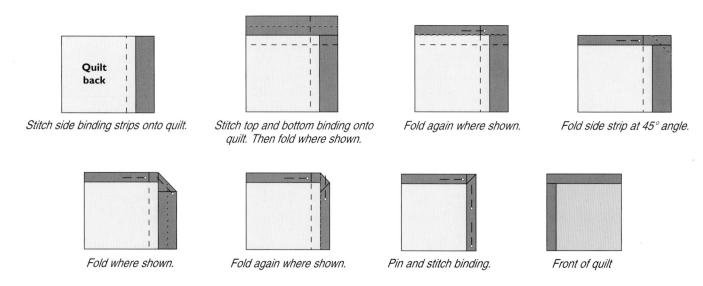

Stitch side binding strips onto quilt.

Stitch top and bottom binding onto quilt. Then fold where shown.

Fold again where shown.

Fold side strip at 45° angle.

Fold where shown.

Fold again where shown.

Pin and stitch binding.

Front of quilt

Fold lines are shown in red.

Projects

No matter the color of your cat, you're sure to find him or her hiding in many of these delightful projects. Pick fabrics to turn any of these cats into *your* cat—right down to the perfect pink for that dear little nose. Add more borders, enlarge or reduce, use that artistic license, and have fun with colors. Put a cat on a pillow. Put a cat on a coat. From wallhangings to bed quilts, these cats are sure to be part of many of your "pet" projects.

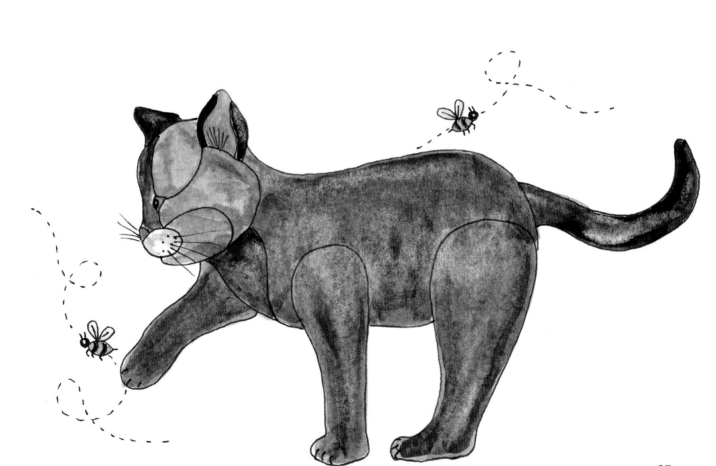

Puss in the Corner

Finished Size: 23½″ × 23½″

MATERIALS

- ⅛ yard of light tan for pieced background
- ¼ yard of tan for pieced background
- 1⅛ yards of muslin for pieced background and backing
- ⅓ yard of print for border
- Selection of fabrics for appliqué
- ⅓ yard for binding
- 26″ × 26″ batting
- Threads to match appliqué fabrics
- Natural color quilting thread
- Embroidery floss: black, brown
- Small piece of faux suede for eyes
- Gel pens for coloring: black, green
- White paint to dot the eyes
- Fabric glue to attach the eyes
- Extras: Carpet thread or waxed linen thread for dimensional whiskers: black

CUTTING

Muslin: Cut 1 square 6½″ × 6½″.
Cut 4 rectangles 4½″ × 6½″.
Cut 20 squares 2½″ × 2½″.
Light tan: Cut 4 rectangles 2½″ × 6½″.
Tan: Cut 16 squares 2½″ × 2½″.
Border: Cut 3 strips 3″ wide, selvage to selvage.
Binding: Cut 4 strips 2″ wide, selvage to selvage.

The background is an 18″ pieced Puss in the Corner block—just right to serve as a home for this contrite kitty. Use quiet colors in the piecing, so the cat remains the central focus.

PIECED BACKGROUND

Make 4 Nine-Patch blocks from the 2½˝ squares; press toward the darker color.

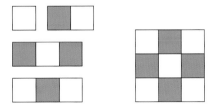

Make 4.

Stitch the light tan rectangles to the muslin rectangles; press toward the darker color.

Make 4.

Stitch the 6½" muslin square and the 8 pieced blocks together to form the pieced background. Press.

Measure the pieced background and trim the border strips to length. Stitch the borders to the background (page 21).

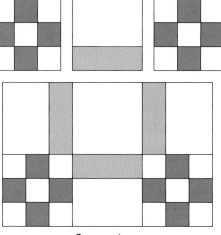

Sew as shown.

APPLIQUÉ

Mark the pattern for the appliqué (pattern on pullout) in the center area of your pieced background. Mark each appliqué piece as well. See the photo (page 27) for placement. Appliqué the cat in the numbered order. Pre-appliqué 22 and 21 onto 20, then 25 and 24 onto 23. Be sure to turn under the edges around the eyes.

DETAILS

See pages 16–17 to make the eyes. I made these eyes round by cutting off the points. Set aside. Fill in the eye area of the appliqué with black pen since the round eyes will allow some background to show. Use black French knots for the muzzle dots. Brown stem stitch is used to make the ear fur. Satin stitch the nostrils in black. Remove any markings. Press. Add the dimensional whiskers (pages 18–19). Layer and baste (pages 22–23).

QUILTING AND FINISHING

Quilt around the cat body parts and the outside of the cat. Echo quilt around the cat once. Quilt in-the-ditch around the pieces and add some diagonal lines through the muslin pieces, marking the lines with masking tape. See the photo for reference. Stitch a line of quilting around the border, 1" in from the edge around the border.

Remove the basting and trim the batting and backing flush with the border. To bind your quilt, measure it, trim the binding strips, and stitch (page 24).

Glue the eyes in place. Allow the glue to dry thoroughly.

Newborns— Gallagher and Sebastian

Finished Size: 16½″ × 14″

MATERIALS

- ⅝ yard of muslin for background and backing
- ⅓ yard of print for border
- Selection of fabrics for appliqué
- ¼ yard for binding
- 19″ × 16″ batting
- Threads to match appliqué fabrics
- Natural color quilting thread
- Embroidery floss: white
- Small piece of faux suede for eyes
- Gel pens for coloring: black, blue, gold
- White paint to dot the eyes
- Fabric glue to attach the eyes

CUTTING

Background: Cut the muslin 12½″ wide × 10″ high. It will be trimmed later.

Border: Cut 2 strips 3½″ wide, selvage to selvage.

Binding: Cut 2 strips 2″ wide, selvage to selvage.

Nothing could be sweeter! These little darlings are made from very simple pieces. A baby-themed fabric would be perfect for the border of this project.

APPLIQUÉ

Mark the pattern for the appliqué. Appliqué the cat on the left first, then
the one on the right. Follow the numbered order of appliqué for each cat.
These little ones are simple. There are no pieces to pre-appliqué.

DETAILS

See pages 16–17 to make 2 sets of eyes. Set aside. Using a single strand of
white, stem stitch the whiskers. Use a black pen for the nostrils and tiny
mouths. Add muzzle dots and toes with colored pen to match each kitten.
Allow to dry.

Remove any markings. Press. Trim to 10½″ wide × 8″ high. Measure and trim the border strips to length (page 21). Stitch the borders to the background. Layer and baste (pages 22–23).

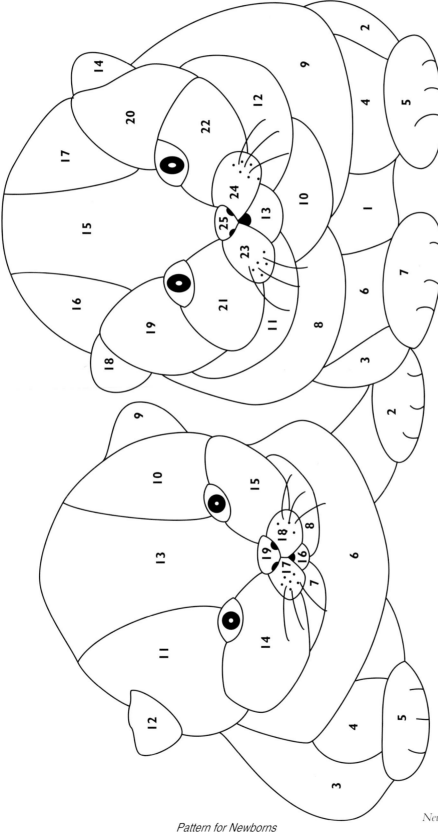

QUILTING AND FINISHING

Quilt around the eye sockets and major body parts, as well as around the outer edge of each kitten. Fill the muslin background with hearts of random sizes and placement. Quilt around the edge of the background and ¼″ into the border. Then, working in rounds, fill the border with random shells.

Remove the basting and trim the batting and backing flush with the border. To bind your quilt, measure it, trim the binding strips, and stitch (page 24).

Glue the eyes in place. Allow the glue to dry thoroughly.

Pattern for Newborns

Newborns—Gallagher and Sebastian **31**

Rainbow Kittens

Finished Size: 22″ × 23″

MATERIALS

- 1⅛ yards of muslin for backgrounds and backing
- ⅓ yard of print for border
- ⅛ yard for sashing
- 4 squares, 1¼″ × 1¼″ each, of 4 colors for pieced center square
- Selection of fabrics for appliqué
- ⅓ yard for binding
- 24″ × 25″ batting
- Threads to match appliqué fabrics
- Natural color quilting thread
- Embroidery floss: black, assorted colors for ears
- Small piece of faux suede for eyes
- Gel pens for coloring: black, green
- White paint to dot the eyes
- Fabric glue to attach the eyes

CUTTING

Background: Cut 4 pieces of muslin, each 10″ wide × 10½″ high. They will be trimmed later.
Sashing: Cut 2 strips 2″ × 8½″ and 2 strips 2″ × 8″.
Border: Cut 3 strips 3″ wide, selvage to selvage.
Binding: Cut 4 strips 2″ wide, selvage to selvage.

This is a great scrappy project. Get out those little pieces you were saving and create these colorful creatures. Pure fun and very cheerful!

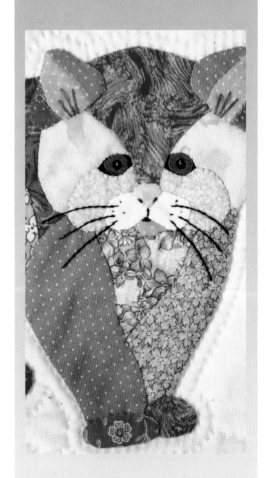

APPLIQUÉ

Mark the pattern for the appliqué. Appliqué each cat in shades of one color in the numbered order. Pre-appliqué 20 and 19 onto 18, then 23 and 22 onto 21. Be sure to turn under the edges around the eyes.

DETAILS

See pages 16–17 to make the eyes. I made these eyes round by cutting off the points. Set aside. Fill in the eye areas of the appliqué with black pen since the round eyes will allow some background to show. Use a black pen for the nostrils and mouths. Embroider the whiskers in stem stitch with a single strand of black. Sew small straight stitches with a single strand of black for the muzzle dots. With 2 strands in coordinating colors, sew some straight stitches in the ears.

Remove any markings. Press. Trim the blocks to 8″ wide × 8½″ high. When trimming, be sure to keep the kittens all positioned the same within their respective backgrounds.

PIECING

Make a center square from the four 1¼″ squares. Press.

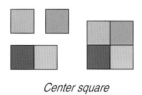

Center square

Piece the top with the sashings and the colored block in the center using a ¼″ seam allowance. Press.

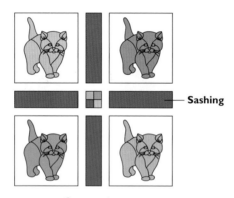

Sew as shown.

Measure the pieced top and trim the border strips to length (page 21). Stitch the borders to the top. Layer and baste (pages 22–23).

QUILTING AND FINISHING

Quilt around each cat and echo once. Quilt around each block's edge and add a single line of shells curving to the inside of the blocks. They are similar in size but not predrawn with any pattern. Use ¾″ masking tape for marking and quilt around the border twice.

Remove the basting and trim the batting and backing flush with the border. To bind your quilt, measure it, trim the binding strips, and stitch (page 24).

Glue the eyes in place. Allow the glue to dry thoroughly.

Pattern for Rainbow Kittens

Snowball in the Strawberry Jar

Finished Size: 17½″ × 20½″

MATERIALS

- ¾ yard of muslin for background and backing
- ¼ yard of print for border
- Selection of fabrics for appliqué
- ¼ yard for binding
- 20″ × 23″ batting
- Threads to match appliqué fabrics
- Natural color quilting thread
- Embroidery floss: gray, green
- Small piece of faux suede for eyes
- Gel pens for coloring: green, black
- White paint to dot the eyes
- Fabric glue to attach the eyes

CUTTING

Background: Cut the muslin 14½″ wide × 17½″ high. It will be trimmed later.
Border: Cut 2 strips 3″ wide, selvage to selvage.
Binding: Cut 3 strips 2″ wide, selvage to selvage.

Surprise! Bet you didn't see me hiding in here! Bright red, ripe strawberries add a bold accent to this design.

APPLIQUÉ

Mark the pattern for the appliqué (pattern on pullout). Appliqué the large piece of the pot first. Then follow the appliqué order. Be sure to turn under the edges around the eyes. Use bias for the stems (pages 14–15). Pre-appliqué 28 and 27 onto 26, then 21 and 22 onto 20. Pre-appliqué the two-piece strawberry leaves, sewing the small piece onto the larger piece.

DETAILS

See pages 16–17 to make the eyes. Set aside. Using a single strand of gray floss, stem stitch the whiskers. Use black pen to mark the toes, muzzle dots, nostrils, and mouth. With green floss, outline the strawberry sepals in stem stitch and fill in with satin stitch.

Remove any markings. Press. Trim to 12½″ wide × 15½″ high. Measure and trim the border strips to length (page 21). Stitch the borders to the background. Layer and baste (pages 22–23).

QUILTING AND FINISHING

Quilt around the cat, jar, fruit with leaves, and the cat's main body parts. Fill the background with leaves randomly scattered. Some simple straight lines finish the border.

Remove the basting and trim the batting and backing flush with the border. To bind your quilt, measure it, trim the binding strips, and stitch (page 24).

Glue the eyes in place. Allow the glue to dry thoroughly.

Buttercup and Spilled Milk

Finished Size: 17½″ × 15″

MATERIALS

- ⅝ yard of muslin for background and backing
- ⅓ yard of print for border
- Selection of fabrics for appliqué
- ¼ yard for binding
- 20″ × 17″ batting
- Threads to match appliqué fabrics
- Natural color quilting thread
- Embroidery floss: brown
- Small piece of faux suede for eyes
- Gel pens for coloring: black, blue
- White paint to dot the eyes
- Fabric glue to attach the eyes

CUTTING

Background: Cut the muslin 13½″ wide × 11″ high. It will be trimmed later.

Border: Cut 2 strips 3½″ wide, selvage to selvage.

Binding: Cut 2 strips 2″ wide, selvage to selvage.

Oops! Well, he certainly looks properly admonished. Or perhaps just upset at his mistake. A cute appliqué piece.

APPLIQUÉ

Mark the pattern for the appliqué (pattern on pullout). Appliqué the floor onto the muslin first, extending the side and bottom edges out into the seam allowance. These edges will be caught in the seam when the borders are added. Follow the numbered order for the rest. Be sure to turn under the edges around the eyes. Pre-appliqué the bowl: 3 onto 2, 4 onto 3, and 5 onto 4. Pre-appliqué 26 onto 25, then 28 onto 27.

DETAILS

See pages 16–17 to make the eyes. Set aside. Using a single strand of brown floss, stem stitch the whiskers. Use a black pen for the mouth, nostrils, and muzzle dots.

Remove any markings. Press. Trim to 11½″ wide × 9″ high. Measure and trim the border strips to length (page 21). Stitch the borders to the background. Layer and baste (pages 22–23).

QUILTING AND FINISHING

Radiate lines out on the floor. Quilt in the eye spaces and around the cat, main body parts, bowl, and milk. Fill the background with spiraling circles of various sizes. Fill the border with some wavy lines.

Remove the basting and trim the batting and backing flush with the border. To bind your quilt, measure it, trim the binding strips, and stitch (page 24).

Glue the eyes in place. Allow the glue to dry thoroughly.

Quilter's Helper

Finished Size: 19½″ × 21″

MATERIALS

- ¾ yard of muslin for background and backing
- ⅓ yard of print for border
- Selection of fabrics for appliqué
- ⅓ yard for binding
- 22″ × 23″ batting
- Threads to match appliqué fabrics
- Natural color quilting thread
- Embroidery floss: brown, red, purple, yellow, green, tan
- Small piece of faux suede for eyes
- Gel pens for coloring: black, green
- White paint to dot the eyes
- Fabric glue to attach the eyes

CUTTING

Background: Cut the muslin 15½″ wide × 17″ high. It will be trimmed later.

Border: Cut 2 strips 3½″ wide, selvage to selvage.

Binding: Cut 4 strips 2″ wide, selvage to selvage.

Appliqué some of your favorite things: sewing notions and a dear friend. Add a few real pins to the cushion to create a great wallhanging for the sewing room.

APPLIQUÉ

Mark the pattern for the appliqué (pattern on pullout). First pre-appliqué the little leaves to the tomato sections. Then appliqué the tomato pincushion to the background. Appliqué the cat in the numbered order. Pre-appliqué 16 onto 15, 18 onto 17, 19 and 20 onto 18, and 22 and 23 onto 21. Remember to turn under the edges around the eyes. Appliqué the spools of thread.

DETAILS

See pages 16–17 to make the eyes. Set aside. With a single strand of brown, stem stitch the whiskers. Single stitches of brown make the muzzle dots. Use straight tan stitches in the ears. A single line of green stem stitch outlines tomato pieces 3 and 5. Stem stitch the thread to match the spool color using a single strand of floss. Black pen colors the holes in the spools.

Remove any markings. Press. Trim to 13½″ wide × 15″ high. Measure and trim the border strips to length (page 21). Stitch the borders to the background. Layer and baste (pages 22–23).

QUILTING AND FINISHING

Quilt around the eye spaces and the main cat body parts. Quilt around the outside of the cat, spools, and pincushion. Break the quilt into sections with straight, double quilt lines. Then fill in the spaces created. I used triangles and echoed curved lines in the outer sections and wavy radiating lines in the central spaces. Feel free to fill in each section differently.

Remove the basting and trim the batting and backing flush with the border. To bind your quilt, measure it, trim the binding strips, and stitch (page 24).

Glue the eyes in place. Allow the glue to dry thoroughly.

Sophie—Just Fishing

Finished Size: 20″ × 21″

MATERIALS

- ¾ yard of muslin for background and backing
- ⅓ yard of print for border
- Selection of fabrics for appliqué
- ⅓ yard for binding
- 22″ × 23″ batting
- Threads to match appliqué fabrics
- Natural color quilting thread
- Embroidery floss: green
- Small piece of faux suede for eyes
- Gel pens for coloring: green, black, orange
- White paint to dot the eyes
- Fabric glue to attach the eyes
- Extras: Waxed linen thread for whiskers: black

CUTTING

Background: Cut the muslin 15″ wide × 16″ high. It will be trimmed later.

Border: Cut 2 strips 4″ wide, selvage to selvage.

Binding: Cut 4 strips 2″ wide, selvage to selvage.

Dimensional whiskers are practically wiggling on this over-curious cat. A simple outline of embroidery created the glass fishbowl.

APPLIQUÉ

Mark the pattern for the appliqué (pattern on pullout). Appliqué the cat. Pre-appliqué 4 onto 3, 16 onto 15, 19 and 18 onto 17, and 21 and 22 onto 20. Remember to turn under the edges around the eyes. Leave the bottom 1½″ of the 2 cat paws, pieces 6 and 7, unstitched. Appliqué them down after the border is attached. (Refer to photo.) Appliqué the fish. Pre-appliqué 3 onto 4. Add the rocks. Pre-appliqué and add the seaweed. Finish with the fishbowl's base. Be sure to extend the bottom of the cat, pieces 1 and 5, and the base of the bowl off the edge into the seam allowance. These edges will be caught in the seam when the borders are added.

DETAILS

See pages 16–17 to make the eyes. Set aside. Mark the nostrils, muzzle dots, cat's mouth, fish mouth, and fish eye ring in black pen. Fill in the fish eye in orange pen and dot with black. Embroider the bowl outline in stem stitch using 2 strands of green.

Remove any markings. Press. Trim to 13″ wide × 14″ high. Be sure to start at the bottom edge when trimming so you will have the raw edges of the appliqué included in the border seam allowance. Measure and trim the border strips to length (page 21). Stitch the borders to the background. Be careful not to catch the unstitched paws in the border seams. Finish appliquéing the paws. Add dimensional whiskers (pages 18–19). Layer and baste (pages 22–23).

QUILTING AND FINISHING

Quilt around the inside of the eye spaces and the major cat body parts. Stitch around the outside of the cat, fish, and bowl. Echo lines out from the bowl and cat 3 times. Add teardrops around the echo lines. Echo outside the drops 2 times. Radiate lines from the last echo to the edge of the muslin. Add some wavy lines and bubbles inside the fishbowl. Quilt the outside edge of the background. Fill the border with random lines from edge to edge, crossing sometimes. Use masking tape for these lines for easy marking.

Remove the basting and trim the batting and backing flush with the border. To bind your quilt, measure it, trim the binding strips, and stitch (page 24).

Glue the eyes in place. Allow the glue to dry thoroughly.

Goldie and the Butterfly—Eyes Open and Eyes Shut

Finished Size: 13½″ × 16″

MATERIALS (FOR ONE DESIGN)

- ⅝ yard of muslin for background and backing
- ¼ yard of print for border
- Selection of fabrics for appliqué
- ¼ yard for binding
- 16″ × 18″ batting
- Threads to match appliqué fabrics
- Natural color quilting thread
- Embroidery floss: black, yellow, brown, green
- Small piece of faux suede for eyes
- Gel pens for coloring: green, black
- White paint to dot the eyes
- Fabric glue to attach the eyes

CUTTING

Background: Cut the muslin 10½″ wide × 13″ high. It will be trimmed later.

Border: Cut 2 strips 3″ wide, selvage to selvage.

Binding: Cut 2 strips 2″ wide, selvage to selvage.

Even the soft landing of a butterfly can wake up this fellow. Make one or both versions of this fun-to-stitch design.

APPLIQUÉ

Mark the pattern for the appliqué. Appliqué the left stem first. Use bias for the stems (pages 14–15). Appliqué the cat following the numbered order. Pre-appliqué 5 onto 4, 11 and 10 onto 9, and 18 and 19 onto 17. Add the stem on the right and all the leaves. Pre-appliqué the two-part leaves, 2 onto 1. Add the flower petals and the butterfly. Turn under the edges on the butterfly wings where they meet the body. This will give a smooth edge to meet the embroidery.

DETAILS

See pages 16–17 to make the eyes for the eyes-open version. Set aside. Use 2 rows of brown stem stitch for the closed eyes. Satin stitch the butterfly body and head in black. With a single strand of black, stem stitch the cat's whiskers and the butterfly's antennae. End each antenna with a French knot. Fill the space in the flower center with yellow French knots. Add one black knot to the center of the yellow ones. Use 2 rows of green stem stitch for the leaf stems.

Remove any markings. Press. Trim to 8½″ wide × 11″ high. Measure and trim the border strips to length (page 21). Stitch the borders to the background. Layer and baste (pages 22–23).

QUILTING AND FINISHING

Quilt around the cat, the eye spaces, and the main cat body parts. Radiate pointed petals out all around the cat. Connect the points with arcs. Echo the arcs 3 times with lines about ½″ apart. Finish the rest of the quilt with random shells.

Remove the basting and trim the batting and backing flush with the border. To bind your quilt, measure it, trim the binding strips, and stitch (page 24).

Glue the eyes in place. Allow the glue to dry thoroughly.

Pattern for Goldie and the Butterfly—Eyes Shut

Pattern for Goldie and the Butterfly—Eyes Open

Jungle Cat

Finished Size: 19¼″ × 14¼″

MATERIALS

- ⅝ yard of muslin for background and backing
- ⅓ yard of print for border
- Selection of fabrics for appliqué
- ¼ yard for binding
- 22″ × 17″ batting
- Threads to match appliqué fabrics
- Natural color quilting thread
- Embroidery floss: black, green
- Small piece of faux suede for eyes
- Gel pens for coloring: black, gold
- White paint to dot the eyes
- Fabric glue to attach the eyes

CUTTING

Background: Cut the muslin 15¼″ wide × 10¼″ high. It will be trimmed later.

Border: Cut 2 strips 3½″ wide, selvage to selvage.

Binding: Cut 2 strips 2″ wide, selvage to selvage.

This quiet kitty is watching the world from a hidden spot in the autumn foliage. I fussy cut some of the leaves from a fall leaf-print fabric.

APPLIQUÉ

Mark the pattern for the appliqué (pattern on pullout). Appliqué the cat first. Pre-appliqué 10 and 11 onto 9, then 24 and 25 onto 23. Be sure to turn under the edges around the eyes. Appliqué the larger stems and then the leaves. The leaf stems will be embroidered. Note when one stem overlaps another for the order of appliqué. The same applies to the leaves. Allow the raw ends of the stems to extend into the outer seam allowance. These will be caught in the seam attaching the borders.

DETAILS

See pages 16–17 to make the eyes. Set aside. Use black pen for the nostrils, mouth, and muzzle dots. Use single-strand stem stitch in black for the whiskers. Using 2 strands of green, embroider a double line of stem stitch for the leaf stems.

Remove any markings. Press. Trim to 13¼″ wide × 8¼″ high. Measure and trim the border strips to length (page 21). Stitch the borders to the background. Layer and baste (pages 22–23).

QUILTING AND FINISHING

Quilt around the leaves, stems, and cat. Stitch around the major cat body parts. Echo out from the appliqué pieces to fill in the small background areas with lines about ¼″ apart. Quilt around the border in straight lines ¾″ apart. Use masking tape to mark these lines easily.

Remove the basting and trim the batting and backing flush with the border. To bind your quilt, measure it, trim the binding strips, and stitch (page 24).

Glue the eyes in place. Allow the glue to dry thoroughly.

All Tangled Up

Finished Size: 22½″ × 17″

MATERIALS

- ⅔ yard of muslin for background and backing
- ⅓ yard of print for border
- Selection of fabrics for appliqué
- ¼ yard for binding
- 25″ × 19″ batting
- Threads to match appliqué fabrics
- Natural color quilting thread
- Embroidery floss: tan
- Small piece of faux suede for eyes
- Gel pens for coloring: blue
- White paint to dot the eyes
- Fabric glue to attach the eyes
- Extras: Cotton crochet yarn in gold and gold metallic thread

CUTTING

Background: Cut the muslin 18¾″ wide × 13″ high. It will be trimmed later.

Border: Cut 2 strips 3½″ wide, selvage to selvage.

Binding: Cut 3 strips 2″ wide, selvage to selvage.

Little pink toes are all tangled up in crochet cotton. This playful cat is embellished with the cotton yarn after the quilting is complete.

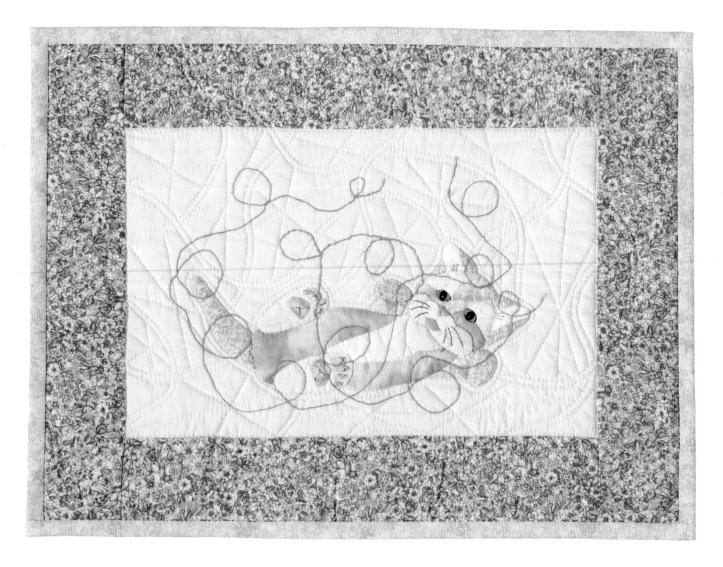

APPLIQUÉ

Mark the pattern for the appliqué (pattern on pullout). Appliqué the cat in order. Pre-appliqué 7 onto 6, 13 and 14 onto 12, and 27 and 28 onto 26. Stitch the foot pads and toes last. Remember to turn under the edges around the eyes.

DETAILS

See pages 16–17 to make the eyes. Set aside. Embroider the whiskers in stem stitch using a single strand of dark tan. Add some straight stitches to the inside of the ears in tan.

Remove any markings. Press. Trim to 16¾″ wide × 11″ high. Measure and trim the border strips to length (page 21). Stitch the borders to the background. Layer and baste (pages 22–23).

QUILTING AND FINISHING

Quilt around the eye spaces and main cat body parts. Echo around the cat once. Quilt around the outside edge of the background. Quilt double lines of curving "yarns" all over the quilt, including the border, creating spaces. Fill in those spaces with X's composed of 3 intersecting lines. Refer to the photo on page 57.

Remove the basting and trim the batting and backing flush with the border. To bind your quilt, measure it, trim the binding strips, and stitch (page 24).

Glue the eyes in place. Allow the glue to dry thoroughly.

EMBELLISHMENTS

Lay gold crochet cotton in random loops on the quilt. Pin in place. With matching metallic thread, stitch over the cotton yarn all along its length to hold it in place. Try not to stitch through all the layers, so your stitches do not come through to the back of the quilt.

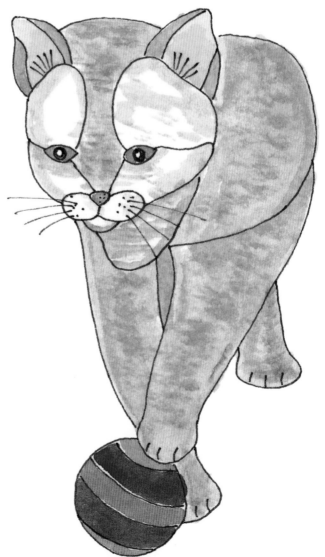

Coco and Polly

Finished Size: 17½″ × 20½″

MATERIALS

- ⅔ yard of muslin for background and backing
- ¼ yard of print for border
- Selection of fabrics for appliqué
- ¼ yard for binding
- 20″ × 23″ batting
- Threads to match appliqué fabrics
- Natural color quilting thread
- Embroidery floss: black, gray, yellow, brown
- Small piece of faux suede for eyes
- Gel pens for coloring: green, black
- White paint to dot the eyes
- Fabric glue to attach the eyes

CUTTING

Background: Cut the muslin 14½″ wide × 17½″ high. It will be trimmed later.

Border: Cut 2 strips 3″ wide, selvage to selvage.

Binding: Cut 3 strips 2″ wide, selvage to selvage.

They're just good friends. They both agree. And we can agree that this project will bring a smile to all.

APPLIQUÉ

Mark the pattern for the appliqué (pattern on pullout). Appliqué the bird first, according to the numbered order. You do not need to turn under the edges around the bird's eye; the eye will be applied on top of the appliqué. Follow the order and appliqué the cat. Pre-appliqué 6 onto 5, then 31 onto 30. Pre-appliqué the 3-piece feather: 2 onto 1, then 3 onto the result. Appliqué the feather on top of the cat.

DETAILS

See pages 16–17 to make the eyes. I made these eyes round by cutting off the points of the corners. Cut a tiny eye for the bird. Use white or cream suede and color the suede with paint or pen. Set all the eyes aside. Color in the cat eye sockets with black pen. With a single strand of black floss, stem stitch the whiskers; add small straight stitches for the muzzle dots and a line of stem stitch down the center of the feather. Satin stitch the nostrils and mouth in black. Echo the black line in the feather with a line of yellow stem stitch. Use gray straight stitches in the cat's ears. Satin stitch the bird's foot in brown. I added a stitch in the corner of the beak for a smile. With a single strand of black, outline the bird's eye.

Remove any markings. Press. Trim to 12½″ wide × 15½″ high. Measure and trim the border strips to length (page 21). Stitch the borders to the background. Layer and baste (pages 22–23).

QUILTING AND FINISHING

Quilt around the cat and bird and around the larger cat body parts. Add a large feather behind the cat. Scatter a handful of circles about and fill in the background with lines curving every which way. Use parallel lines approximately ¾″ apart around the border. Use masking tape to make this marking easy.

Remove the basting and trim the batting and backing flush with the border. To bind your quilt, measure it, trim the binding strips, and stitch (page 24).

Glue the eyes in place. Allow the glue to dry thoroughly.

Cat and Mouse

Finished Size: 26¼″ × 22¼″

MATERIALS

- 1¼ yards of muslin for background and backing
- ½ yard of print for border
- Selection of fabrics for appliqué
- ⅓ yard for binding
- 29″ × 25″ batting
- Threads to match appliqué fabrics
- Natural color quilting thread
- Embroidery floss: brown, black, gray
- Gel pens for coloring: black, gold
- White paint to dot the eye
- Black seed bead for mouse's eye
- 60 red 4mm beads for berries

CUTTING

Background: Cut the muslin 20¼″ wide × 16¼″ high. It will be trimmed later.

Border: Cut 3 strips 4½″ wide, selvage to selvage.

Binding: Cut 4 strips 2″ wide, selvage to selvage.

Some raspberry-red beads compose the berry of contention between these two characters. The mouse is a bit of a challenge, since it has some small pieces to appliqué.

APPLIQUÉ

Mark the pattern for the appliqué (pattern on pullout). Appliqué the small stems first, then the main stem. Use bias (pages 14–15). Add the leaves. Appliqué the mouse in the numbered order. Use tiny bias for the tail (page 15). Appliqué the cat, beginning with the tail. Mark the pupil on the green eye fabric before appliquéing it. Pre-appliqué the ears: 14 onto 13, then 15 onto 13. Complete the cat in the numbered order.

DETAILS

Embroider the cat whiskers in stem stitch with a single strand of brown. Use black single-strand stem stitch for the mouse whiskers. Place a dot of white paint on the pupil of the cat's eye. Mark the cat's toes with black pen. Fill in the eye area of the mouse with gold gel pen. Stem stitch around the inside edge of the mouse's eye using a single strand of black. Make a few straight stitches inside the mouse's ear in gray.

Remove any markings. Press. Trim to 18¼″ wide × 14¼″ high. Measure and trim the border strips to length (page 21). Stitch the borders to the background. Layer and baste (pages 22–23).

QUILTING AND FINISHING

Quilt radiating lines in sections going in various directions, marking the lines with masking tape. Outline quilt around the mouse, leaves, and cat and around the larger cat body parts.

Remove the basting and trim the batting and backing flush with the border. To bind your quilt, measure it, trim the binding strips, and stitch (page 24).

EMBELLISHMENTS

Sew a black seed bead in the mouse's eye. Stitch a cluster of 12 red beads at each stem end and between the mouse and cat to form raspberries.

Neffie's Silhouette

Finished Size: 21½″ by 24″

MATERIALS

- 1¼ yards of muslin for background and backing
- ⅓ yard of print for border
- Selection of fabrics for appliqué
- ⅓ yard for binding
- 24″ × 26″ batting
- Threads to match appliqué fabrics
- Natural color quilting thread
- Embroidery floss: green

CUTTING

Background: Cut the muslin 16½″ wide × 19″ high. It will be trimmed later.

Border: Cut 2 strips 4″ wide, selvage to selvage.

Binding: Cut 4 strips 2″ wide, selvage to selvage.

APPLIQUÉ

Mark the pattern for the appliqué (pattern on pullout). Appliqué following the numbered order. The small branch on top of the cat is sewn in part before the cat. The part under the large branch is sewn first; the rest is sewn after the cat is sewn down.

DETAILS

Embroider the little leaf stems with green stem stitch.

Remove any markings. Press. Trim to 14½″ wide × 17″ high. Measure and trim the border strips to length (page 21). Stitch the borders to the background. Layer and baste (pages 22–23).

A simple design creates an elegant scene. You will enjoy stitching this motif.

QUILTING AND FINISHING

Cut a circle template 3″ in diameter. Pin and quilt around this template all over the quilt, overlapping the circles to create an interesting design. Do not quilt in the appliqué itself.

Remove the basting and trim the batting and backing flush with the border. To bind your quilt, measure it, trim the binding strips, and stitch (page 24).

Whiskers Pin

Finished Size: 3″ × 2¾″

MATERIALS

- Scrap of muslin for background
- Selection of fabrics for appliqué and backing
- Scrap of batting: light cotton
- Threads to match appliqué fabrics
- Embroidery floss: brown
- Small piece of faux suede for eyes
- Gel pens for coloring: green, black
- White paint to dot the eyes
- Fabric glue to attach the eyes
- Extras: Waxed linen thread for whiskers: black
- Pin for back

CUTTING

Background: Cut a piece of muslin 5″ × 5″. It will be trimmed later.

Any cat face can make a pin. It is appliquéd in the usual fashion on muslin first. Keep the outer edge of the design simple to make any motif "pinable."

APPLIQUÉ

Mark the pattern for the appliqué. Appliqué the cat head onto the muslin. Pre-appliqué 13 and 12 onto 11, then 16 and 15 onto 14. Be sure to turn under the edges that meet the eye area.

DETAILS

See pages 16–17 to make the eyes. Make them round by cutting off the corners. Set aside. Fill in the eye spaces on the muslin with black pen. Use the same pen for the nostrils, muzzle dots, and mouth. Use brown straight stitches in the ears.

Remove any markings. Press. Add the whiskers. Split the waxed linen. Using 2 strands of linen, sew 3 whiskers on each side (pages 18–19). With a small piece of masking tape, hold the whiskers in the center of the face so they will not be caught in the seam allowance.

FINISHING

Trim around the face, leaving an extra ½″ of the background fabric for the seam allowance. With right sides together, put the appliquéd head and the backing together on top of a piece of light cotton batting. With the back side of the appliquéd head facing up, stitch the layers together using the perimeter appliqué stitches as a guide. Sew just outside or on top of these stitches with a running stitch. Leave a space open at the bottom for turning. Trim the allowance close to the seam and clip at the ears. Turn right side out. Stitch or glue the opening closed. Free the whiskers from the masking tape. Press. Glue the eyes in place and sew the pin onto the back.

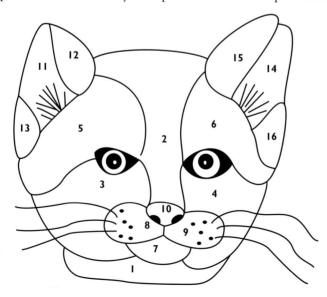

Pattern for Whiskers Pin

Boo, the Halloween Calico

Finished Size: 21½″ × 20¾″

MATERIALS

- 1¼ yards of muslin for background and backing
- ¼ yard of print for border
- Selection of fabrics for appliqué
- ⅓ yard for binding
- 24″ × 23″ batting
- Threads to match appliqué fabrics
- Natural color quilting thread
- Embroidery floss: black
- Gel pens for coloring: green, black, brown
- White paint to dot the eyes

CUTTING

Background: Cut the muslin 18½″ wide × 17½″ high. It will be trimmed later.

Border: Cut 2 strips 3″ wide, selvage to selvage.

Binding: Cut 4 strips 2″ wide, selvage to selvage.

This cat is sewn using my Appliqué-Inside-the-Lines technique. The simple stem-stitch outline is embroidered first and then filled in with simple appliqué—a great look. You get more detail with less appliqué.

APPLIQUÉ

Mark and embroider all the outlines of the cat (pattern on pullout). Stem stitch using 2 strands of black floss. Remove any markings and press. Cut out a template the exact size of each appliqué section. Lay each template on top of your chosen appliqué fabric and cut out each shape, leaving a $\frac{3}{16}$" turn-under allowance. Lay each appliqué piece over the embroidered section. Pin to hold in place and appliqué. As you turn under the allowance, allow $\frac{1}{8}$" or so of the background fabric to be exposed between the appliqué's edge and the embroidery. Fill in the sections to be appliquéd in any order.

DETAILS

Fill in the eye areas with gel pens—green for the iris, black for the pupil, and brown for the outside of the eye. Place a white paint dot in each pupil. Add a few black dots to the muzzle.

Remove any markings. Press. Trim to $16\frac{1}{2}$" wide × $15\frac{3}{4}$" high. Measure and trim the border strips to length (page 21). Stitch the borders to the background. Layer and baste (pages 22–23).

QUILTING AND FINISHING

Quilt around the appliqué pieces in the space between the appliqué and the embroidery. Fill in the background with stems and leaves. Echo out from the leaves to fill in any remaining background area. Quilt around the edge of the muslin and 1" into the border. Mark with masking tape to make this simple.

Remove the basting and trim the batting and backing flush with the border. To bind your quilt, measure it, trim the binding strips, and stitch (page 24).

About the Author

As in her other favorite books, Carol Armstrong gathers her inspiration from the world around her. She and her cabinetmaker husband enjoy a creative, homestead lifestyle in Michigan where long, snowy winters give her lots of time for quilting and creating.

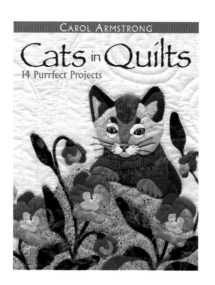

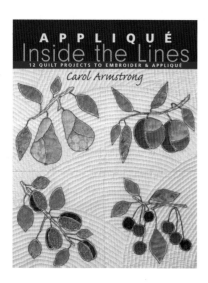